"Not even the Emerald Isle itself was as green as the grass that grew in Ebbets Field."

—Duke Snider

Stewart, Tabori & Chang
New York

101 Reasons to Love the™
DODGERS

Ron Green, Jr.

Introduction

Several years ago at the Atlantic Coast Conference basketball tournament, I was standing with a friend of mine whose memory of our youth in the 1960s remains clearer than my memory of yesterday. We were too young in the '60s to understand the summer of love, the fighting in the streets, and Vietnam — but we understood perfectly what Sandy Koufax meant.

Although we were both New York Yankees fans — it was impossible not to be captivated by Mickey Mantle as a 10-year-old growing up in North Carolina — the Los Angeles Dodgers were our other team because of Koufax, Don Drysdale, and those brilliantly white uniforms with the Dodger blue trim.

SANDY KOUFAX pitcher

As my friend and I were talking, a man with graying hair walked past. He wore jeans and was by himself. Like thousands of others, he was there for the best conference basketball tournament in the land.

"That's Sandy Koufax," I told my friend.

He looked at the man for a minute and wasn't convinced. "Are you sure?" my friend asked.

"Positive," I told him. "I met him last year when he sat beside me at the NCAA tournament. He's a really nice man."

My friend looked at Koufax as he walked away. "It's like seeing one of the Beatles," my friend said.

To us, it was, and I'm sure it would be the same for thousands of others who for generations have affixed their allegiance to the Dodgers.

From Brooklyn to Chavez Ravine, from the Bridegrooms to Eric Gagne, the Dodgers have been an enduringly successful part of the American sports landscape. Much of baseball's history is colored in Dodger blue. The franchise was part of the glory days in New York, when the Giants and Yankees also owned a piece of the great city's heart.

The Dodgers and Branch Rickey gave us Jackie Robinson, assuring that the game and society would never be the same. Although it broke the heart of millions when it headed west, the franchise changed the professional sports map forever with its move to Los Angeles.

The Dodgers have given us Koufax' brilliance, Drysdale's toughness, Orel Hershiser's shutout streak, Tommy Lasorda's chatter, Fernandomania, the Garvey-Lopes-Russell-Cey infield, Kirk Gibson's home run, Dodger dogs, and so much more.

What baseball does best is paint the color into our lives. It's shared by fathers and sons, brothers and sisters, the young and the old. It gives you moments to remember and people to remember them with. And when Sandy Koufax walks past, it gives you the chills all over again.

1 The Bridegrooms

In addition to having one of the great nicknames ever, the Bridegrooms knew their way around a baseball field. The team originated in 1884 as a member of the American Association and then joined the National League in 1890, immediately winning the championship, and posting an 86–43 record. Why the Bridegrooms? Because seven of the team's players were married in 1888, most of them around the same time.

George Pinckney

2 George Pinckney

From September 21, 1885, until May 1, 1890, Pinckney played every inning in 570 games, a streak that went unbroken for nearly a century.

3 Tripleheader Sweep

The Bridegrooms pulled it off, beating Pittsburgh three times on September 1, 1890.

4 The Brickyard

Back before relief pitchers became specialists, William "Brickyard" Kennedy was a bull on the mound. He won 177 games in his Brooklyn career, including four seasons of 20 or more wins, and showed his toughness on May 30, 1893. That's when Kennedy pitched and won both ends of a doubleheader against Louisville, allowing only eight hits over two games — thus becoming the first major-league pitcher to win two games on the same day after the mound was moved back to 60 feet 6 inches from the plate.

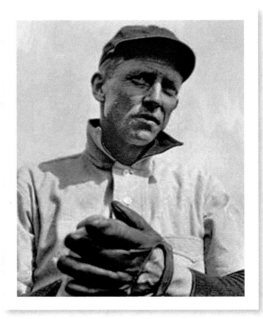

Brickyard Kennedy

5 Hanlon's Superbas

In the late 1800s and early 1900s, one of the most popular troupes on Broadway went by the name Hanlon's Superbas. Not surprisingly, when manager Ned Hanlon led his Brooklyn team to the National League pennant in 1899 and again in 1900, it came to be known as Hanlon's Superbas, too—though those Superbas never played on Broadway.

6 Wee Willie Keeler

When asked once why he was such a good hitter, Wee Willie Keeler famously gave a brilliant answer. "I hit 'em where they ain't," he said.

Keeler, who was born in Brooklyn, did it better than most. In his four full seasons with Brooklyn, from 1899 to 1902, he never hit lower than .333. An excellent bunter, Keeler hit .341 for his career, the 12th-best career batting average ever. His 44-game hitting streak in 1897 is still the second longest in major-league history, tied with Pete Rose for the National League record. As for the nickname, it was obvious—Keeler stood only 5-foot-4.

Wee Willie Keeler

Ned Hanlon

7 Four Triples

The Superbas did it in the third inning of a 9–8 win at Pittsburgh on August 23, 1902, an achievement that is still tied for the major-league record for triples in a game.

8 Tim Jordan

Jordan led the National League in home runs when he hit 12 in 1908. It is noteworthy not so much for what Jordan did, but for the fact that it was 96 years before another Dodger would lead the league in home runs. Adrian Beltre took the honors in 2004, when he hit 48 dingers.

JORDAN, BROOKLYN

Original artwork by Andy Jurinko

9 Ebbets Field

One of the most famous ballparks in history was situated in the Flatbush section of Brooklyn, bordered by Bedford Avenue, Sullivan Street, Franklin Avenue, and Montgomery Street. The area around Ebbets Field was known as "Pig Town," and the ballpark was built on an old garbage dump after team owner Charles Ebbets determined his club couldn't continue to play in Washington Park. Ebbets Field had a capacity of 18,000, but 25,000 spectators jammed themselves in on opening day, April 9, 1913. The ballpark had its own charm, including the right-field wall with multiple angles that always kept outfielders guessing, and a hole in the right-center-field wall that allowed kids to look in on games for free. The Dodgers played here through 1957, before moving west to Los Angeles.

10 Wilbert Robinson

It is quite a tribute to a manager when the team he leads adopts his name as its nickname. That's what happened when Wilbert Robinson managed Brooklyn from 1914 through 1931: the team came to be known as the Robins.

A catcher in his playing days with Baltimore, when he once had seven hits in a nine-inning game, Robinson learned to manage working under the legendary John McGraw for the rival Giants. When "Uncle Robbie" took over in Brooklyn, the Robins made World Series appearances in 1916 and 1920.

11 The Flying Grapefruit

In a spring-training stunt in 1915, Brooklyn manager Wilbert Robinson attempted to catch a baseball dropped from an airplane. Unbeknownst to Robinson, the players had replaced the baseball with a grapefruit. When Robinson attempted to catch the grapefruit, it exploded upon hitting his glove, covering the shocked manager with bits of grapefruit. Robinson was knocked to the ground and thought he had been seriously injured.

"Jesus, I'm killed. I'm blind. It's broke open my chest," Robinson reportedly screamed before realizing he'd been the victim of a practical joke.

"Robbie was a rule-of-thumb manager, a gentle Falstaff, who could get more out of less material than any manager before or since."

— Tom Meany

12 Zack Wheat

Wheat earned a place in the Baseball Hall of Fame as an outfielder who was one of the great hitters of his time. He joined the Dodgers in 1909 and played through 1926, setting team records that still stand. Wheat remains the Dodgers' career leader in hits (2,804), doubles, triples, and total bases. Greatly admired as a person, Wheat was renowned as a hitter, collecting 200 or more hits in three seasons and stringing together three straight years (1923–25) when he hit better than .350.

13 Casey Stengel

Stengel was hugely popular in Brooklyn, where he helped the Dodgers reach the 1916 World Series. He held the distinction of hitting the first home run out of Ebbets Field, but he was traded to Pittsburgh in late 1917, a move that disappointed many Brooklyn fans. When Stengel returned to Ebbets Field in 1918, he was greeted by an enormous ovation. Stengel, ever the showman, tipped his cap to the crowd—and a sparrow flew out.

"I was not successful as a ballplayer, as it was a game of skill."

— Casey Stengel

Casey Stengel

14 The Trolley Dodgers

In the area surrounding Eastern Park in Brooklyn (the team home in 1891–97), trolley cars rolled through the streets, forcing pedestrians to pay attention as they walked. It led to the Trolley Dodgers nickname, which was eventually shortened to Dodgers.

15 Dodger Blue

If you're looking for the right mix, try these combinations: the hex triplet code is 1E90FF, and the red, green, blue mix is 30, 144, 255. That's computer code for color blending. To Dodgers fans, it's simply the prettiest shade of blue anywhere.

16 The Fans

There are, literally, millions of them. They live in Los Angeles and Oxnard and Malibu. They live throughout California, across the country, and around the world. More than 2.7 million people annually visit Dodger Stadium, and they're just a fraction of the devoted fan base that call the Dodgers their team.

TICKET HOLDERS
LOWER TIER BOXES
LOWER RESERVED SEATS · BOXES 1 to 9
ENTER HERE
GATES 6 & 7 ON LEFT
GATES 8 & 9 ON RIGHT

17 A Fast One

On September 21, 1919, the Robins needed just 55 minutes to beat the Cincinnati Reds 3–1 in a nine-inning game.

18 The Longest Game(s)

The first marathon came on May 1, 1920, in Boston against the Braves, and it was a 1–1 tie that lasted 26 innings. Remarkably, both starting pitchers— Brooklyn's Leon Cadore and Boston's Joe Oeschger—went the distance.

But there was more to come. Much more. The following day, the Dodgers lost a 13-inning game, 4–3, to Philadelphia in Brooklyn, and a day later, the Dodgers were back in Boston, where they played 19 more innings, losing 2–1—in all, three games that lasted a total of 58 innings—the equivalent of nearly six and a half nine-inning games.

Leon Cadore

Hy Myers,
Wilbert Robinson,
and mascot

19 The World Series Unassisted Triple Play

It was October 10, Game 5 of the 1920 World Series, and the Dodgers had two men on base in the fifth inning against the Cleveland Indians. Dodgers pitcher Clarence Mitchell was at bat and lined a shot that was snared by Indians second baseman Billy Wambsganss. He stepped on second base to retire Brooklyn's Pete Kilduff, then tagged out Otto Miller, who was running from first on the line drive. One, two, three. The Dodgers had achieved a dubious place in history.

UNASSISTED TRIPLE PLAY

CLARENCE MITCHELL 10/10/20
BROOKLYN DODGERS – BATTER

20 Burleigh Grimes

In a long, outstanding career, Grimes — nick-named "Ol' Stubblebeard" because he refused to shave on days he started — pitched for seven different franchises but had some of his greatest success for the Dodgers between 1918 and 1926. Grimes had a 23–11 record when the Dodgers reached the 1920 World Series, one of four times he won at least 21 games for the team. He was known for his spitball, and when baseball banned the pitch in 1920, Grimes was one of 17 pitchers exempted from the ban.

"I was a real bastard when I played."

—Burleigh Grimes

Burleigh Grimes
and Van Mungo

21 Dazzy Vance

Vance owns a distinctive place in the history of the franchise. A great character once described by *The Sporting News* as "wild as a vodka-soaked Bolshevik in front of a red flag," Vance posted double-figure victories in 10 of his 11 seasons with the Dodgers. His 28 wins led the National League in 1924, as did his 22 wins the next season. For seven straight seasons beginning in 1922, Vance led the National League in strikeouts, twice leading the league in earned run average.

Here's how good Vance was: in consecutive starts in 1925, he pitched a one-hitter and a no-hitter to beat Philadelphia 1–0 and 10–1.

"I like to see a fastball pitcher like Vance wild. It gives the batters something to think about."

—Wilbert Robinson

Clise Dudley

22 Milt Stock's Run

Beginning in late June 1925, Stock had at least four hits in four straight games, a modern record.

23 Clise Dudley's Debut

A relief pitcher, Dudley stepped to the plate in a major-league game for the first time on April 27, 1929. Dudley hit the first pitch ever thrown to him out of the park for a home run, the first time a player hit a home run on the first pitch thrown to him in his career.

24 Dem Bums

During the long drought years between 1921 and 1938, the Dodgers came to be known as "Dem Bums" thanks to a cartoon drawn by Willard Mullin of the *New York World-Telegram*. Mullin was taking a cab home from a Dodgers game when the driver asked him, "How'd our bums do today?" Mullin immortalized the moment in a cartoon, drawing a character to represent "Dem Bums." It became such a part of Dodgers lore that the character landed on the cover of the team's yearbook in 1955.

25 Babe Ruth

His glory days were over when the Babe put on the Brooklyn Dodgers' uniform in 1938. Ruth had retired from playing baseball in 1935 with his name on virtually every significant hitting record in the game. Despite his lavish lifestyle, he had plenty of money, played golf regularly, and was part of the first class of players inducted into the new Baseball Hall of Fame in 1936.

But the Babe missed being on the field. When Dodgers general manager Larry MacPhail offered Ruth the chance to coach first base, Ruth, who wanted to manage a major-league team, thought it might be his chance to take over the Dodgers. However, MacPhail had already determined the manager's job was going to Leo Durocher. Ruth joined the Dodgers in June and made it until the end of the season. That's when his Dodgers days — and his days in a baseball uniform — came to an end.

Burleigh Grimes, Babe Ruth, and Leo Durocher

26 Larry MacPhail

Hired in 1938 as the team's executive vice president, MacPhail wasted no time putting his own touch on the Dodgers. He improved Ebbets Field and hired Red Barber to broadcast Dodgers games, despite an agreement with the other New York teams not to put their games on the radio.

MacPhail had a knack for timing, too. He arranged Brooklyn's first night baseball game on June 15, 1938. It just so happened to be the game when Johnny Vander Meer pitched his second consecutive no-hitter. It was also MacPhail who, that same season, put Babe Ruth in a uniform for the last time, signing him to be a first-base coach for the Dodgers.

27 Yellow Baseballs

Not every one of MacPhail's ideas worked. In August 1938, he introduced baseballs dyed dandelion yellow, but the sunny spheres were used for just three games before the idea was abandoned.

"There is a thin line between genius and insanity, and in Larry's case it was sometimes so thin you could see him drifting back and forth."

—Leo Durocher

Larry MacPhail

28 Pete Reiser

Few players have ever played with the reckless abandon that characterized Reiser's career. By most accounts, Reiser had to be carried off the field 11 times after crashing into the wall chasing fly balls. One collision was so violent that Reiser was given last rites by a priest, though he survived to play again.

A great talent, Reiser was the National League's youngest batting champion when he led the league with a .343 average in 1941. He stole home seven times in one season, and he had a lasting impact on baseball. Many consider Reiser the reason outfields now have warning tracks and many ballparks now have padded walls.

Dolph Camilli;
1941 team, right

29 Dolph Camilli

Camilli's big season—1941, when he was the National League's Most Valuable Player—coincided with the Dodgers' first pennant in 21 years. General manager Larry MacPhail had acquired Camilli specifically to reenergize a lagging franchise, and it paid off handsomely in '41 when the big first baseman hit a league-leading 34 home runs and drove in 120 runs. That helped offset Camilli's 115 strikeouts as he epitomized the notion of a free swinger.

30 The Parade

After the Dodgers won the 1941 National League pennant, a parade was held in their honor through the streets of Brooklyn. A crowd estimated at more than one million people turned out to cheer their heroes. Unfortunately, the crosstown Yankees would win the World Series over the Dodgers, 4 games to 1.

31 Branch Rickey

Rickey was never a great player or manager, but he became one of baseball's most influential people. Although he built his early reputation with the Cardinals, where he was credited with inventing baseball's farm system, Rickey's most profound impact came during his time as the Dodgers' president and general manager from 1942 through 1950. That's when Rickey pioneered the use of statistics in the game and helped make batting helmets and batting cages part of baseball's furniture.

Then, of course, there was Rickey's so-called "Great Experiment," when he broke baseball's color barrier by signing Jackie Robinson to a professional contract in 1945, and then bringing him up to the Dodgers two years later. Rickey later became the first executive to draft a Hispanic, a promising young outfielder named Roberto Clemente.

"Ethnic prejudice has no place in sports, and baseball must recognize that truth if it is to maintain stature as a national game."

—Branch Rickey

32 Nice Guys Finish Last

Dodgers manager Leo Durocher uttered what became known as the classic line, "Nice guys finish last," on July 5, 1946.

33 Red Barber and Ernie Harwell

Both Hall of Fame announcers spent parts of their careers calling Dodgers games. Barber was the play-by-play man for 15 years starting in 1939, using his down-home style to tell the story of each game. Barber, who later went on to call New York Yankees games, popularized the saying "in the catbird seat."

Harwell, best known as the voice of the Detroit Tigers for more than five decades, is the only announcer known to have been part of a trade. When Branch Rickey wanted to hire Harwell to announce Dodgers games in 1948, he had to pry Harwell away from WSB in Atlanta. That meant agreeing to trade minor-league catcher Cliff Dapper to the Atlanta Crackers for the rights to Harwell.

"When I'm talking to a large audience, I imagine that I'm talking to a single person."

—Red Barber

Leo Durocher and friends; Red Barber, inset

34 Cookie's Double

The Dodgers were one out away from being no-hit in Game 4 of the 1947 World Series at Ebbets Field when Cookie Lavagetto ripped a two-run, pinch-hit double off Yankees pitcher Bill Bevens to win the game, 3–2. It was his last career hit and Bevens' last game. Both players' careers ended with the Yankees' victory in Game 7.

Cookie Lavagetto, left, and former Yankees pitcher Bill Bevens, having some fun in 1947, after their playing days were over

35 Jackie Robinson

The man who broke major-league baseball's color barrier became an iconic figure not just for his impact on society and sports, but for his transcendent talents on the diamond. Robinson understood the hateful challenge he faced and handled it with dignity from the moment he set foot on Ebbets Field on April 15, 1947.

In Robinson's 10 seasons with the Dodgers, the team won six National League pennants, a testament to his skills. He was Rookie of the Year in 1947 and the National League's Most Valuable Player in 1949, when he hit .342, drove in 124 runs, and stole 37 bases. Robinson's speed and daring allowed him to steal home 19 times in his career. His achievements were so impressive and historic that his number, 42, has been retired throughout baseball.

36 Ebony and Ivory

When Jackie Robinson broke baseball's color barrier, the Southern-born Pee Wee Reese was there to help him. The Dodgers shortstop saw the storm swirling around Robinson and worked to ease the transition. When Robinson walked into the Dodgers locker room for the first time, Reese walked over and shook his hand, welcoming him in an uncomfortable situation. When a petition began circulating among players in the locker room calling for Robinson's removal from the club, Reese stopped it. And when fans in Cincinnati began heckling Robinson, Reese walked over from his spot at shortstop and draped his arm around his teammate's shoulder to show his support.

37 Pee Wee Reese

Reese was the quiet captain of the Dodgers during the team's exceptional run in the 1950s, playing shortstop with style and grace. He was an outstanding defender who teamed with second baseman Jackie Robinson to form a great double-play combination. Reese was adept at getting on base, drawing more than 1,200 walks in his career, which helped the Dodgers win seven pennants in his 16 seasons. Reese also played every inning of every game in seven World Series.

38 Pee Wee's Big Adventure

On May 21, 1952, in the first inning of a 19–1 win over Cincinnati, Reese tied a major-league record by reaching base safely three times as the Dodgers scored 15 runs before the Reds retired the side for the first time.

Jackie Robinson,
Pee Wee Reese,
and Gil Hodges

The 1952 World Series starting lineup: Billy Cox, third base; Pee Wee Reese, shortstop; Duke Snider, center field; Jackie Robinson, second base; Roy Campanella, catcher; Andy Pafko, left field; Gil Hodges, first base; Carl Furillo, right field; and Joe Black, pitcher

39 The Boys of Summer

They included Jackie Robinson, Pee Wee Reese, Roy Campanella, Gil Hodges, Carl Furillo, Don Newcombe, Carl Erskine, Jim Gilliam, Duke Snider, Preacher Roe, and Clem Labine. Their story was captured forever by author Roger Kahn in *The Boys of Summer*, widely acknowledged as one of the great sports books ever written.

40 The 1950s

They were happy days for the Dodgers, who won five National League pennants (1952, '53, '55, '56, '59) and two world championships ('55 and '59). In eight of 10 seasons in the era of bobby socks and poodle skirts, the Dodgers didn't finish lower than second, winning 913 games, the most in any decade for the franchise.

"You may glory in a team triumphant ... but you fall in love with a team in defeat."

— Roger Kahn

Ralph Branca

41 Bill Sharman's Ejection

Bill Sharman would become a basketball Hall of Famer, but he also owns a unique distinction in baseball history. On September 27, 1951, Sharman—in uniform as a member of the Dodgers after being called up from the minors—was thrown out of the game. He ended up never playing in a major-league game, making him the only player thrown out of a game without ever playing in any.

42 The Shot Heard 'Round the World

Sometimes love hurts. Dodgers fans had their hearts broken on the 3rd of October, 1951, when the Giants' Bobby Thomson hit his famous home run off Ralph Branca. What at one point had been a 13 1/2-game lead in the National League was all gone then, though the Dodgers had a piece of baseball history.

"It was a fastball up and in, and ... the way he swung at the ball, and to hit the ball under those extenuating circumstances, under that pressure, he did a hell of a job."

—Ralph Branca on Bobby Thomson's home run

Bill Sharman

43 60–17

That was the Dodgers' home record in 1953 at Ebbets Field, the best home record for any team until the schedule was expanded to 81 home games.

44 Johnny Podres' Seventh Game

It was October 4, 1955, Game 7 of the World Series against the Yankees, who had already beaten the Dodgers in five previous Series. The Dodgers had never won a Series in seven trips, and their one-game shot rested on the shoulders of their 23-year-old pitcher who had beaten the Yankees 8–3 in Game 3. With more than 62,000 fans jammed into Yankee Stadium, Podres went the distance and delivered the Dodgers their first world championship with a 2–0 win. Delirious Brooklynites celebrated through the night.

45 Roy Campanella

There haven't been many like "Campy." He played 10 seasons for the Dodgers, starting in 1948, and he put together a career that still sparkles. Three times — 1951, 1953, and 1955 — Campanella was the National League's Most Valuable Player. He hit 242 career home runs and was the first black catcher in the major leagues. When he was inducted into the Baseball Hall of Fame in 1969, Campy had done it all.

46 93,103

That's how many fans turned out at Los Angeles Memorial Coliseum on May 7, 1959, to honor Roy Campanella after a broken neck suffered in a 1958 automobile accident tragically ended his career — still the largest crowd in major-league baseball history.

"I never want to quit playing ball. They'll have to cut this uniform off of me to get me out of it."

— Roy Campanella

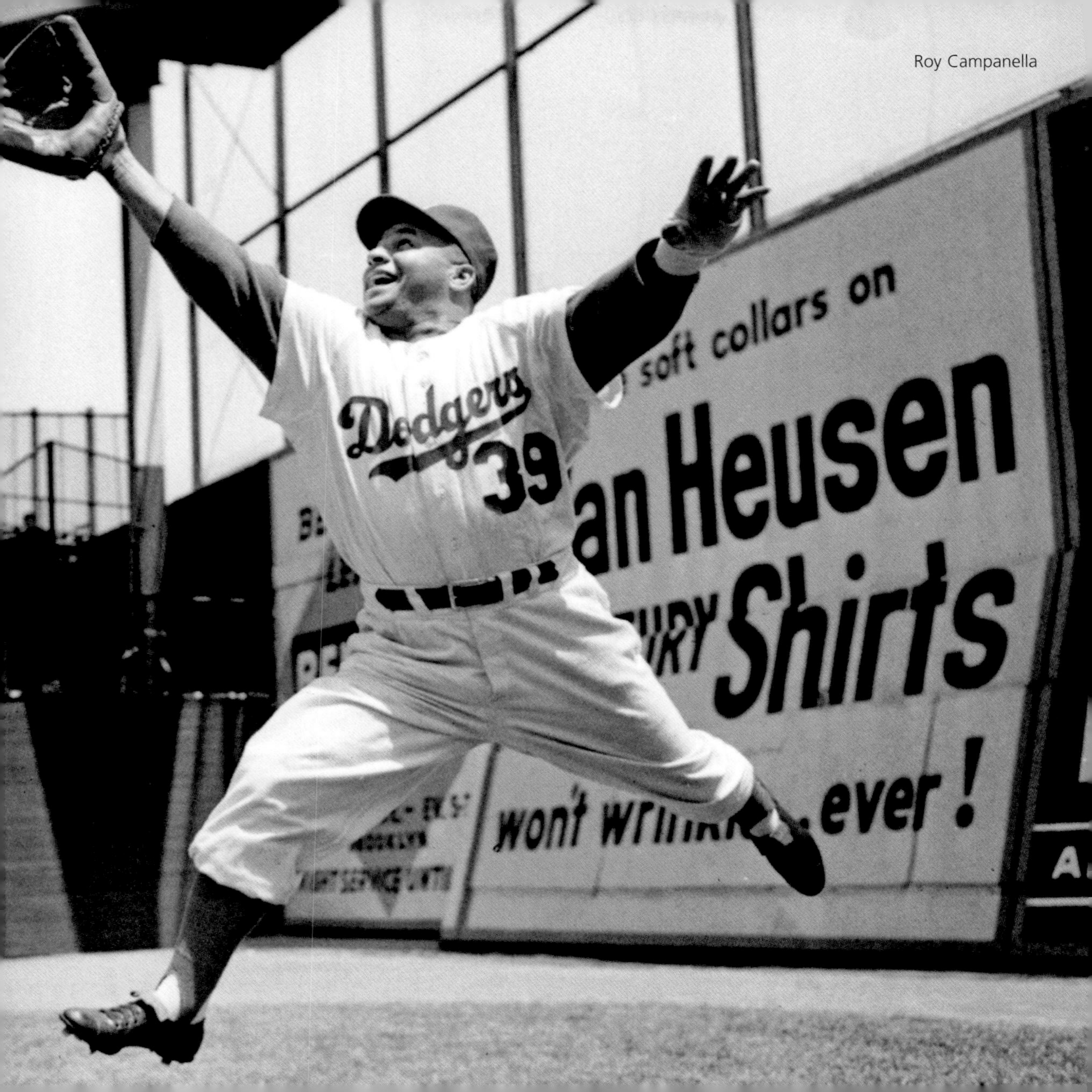

Roy Campanella

47 Duke Snider

The Duke of Flatbush had a classic swing, and it produced classic results for the Hall of Famer. A left-handed-hitting center fielder, Snider smashed 407 career home runs and drove in 1,333 runs. During one stretch, between 1953 and 1957, Snider hit 40 or more home runs in five consecutive seasons.

Snider was part of a golden age of outfielders in New York during the 1950s, when Mickey Mantle and Willie Mays also played in the city. No one, however, hit more home runs or drove in more runs in that decade than Snider.

"Swing hard, in case they throw the ball where you're swinging."

—Duke Snider

48 Gil Hodges

The first baseman was a fixture with the Dodgers through the 1950s, when Hodges' power and style helped define the franchise. He was an eight-time All-Star who hit 370 career home runs while playing in seven World Series with the Dodgers. Hodges' greatest achievement, however, may have come in 1969, when he managed the Amazin' Mets to their first world championship.

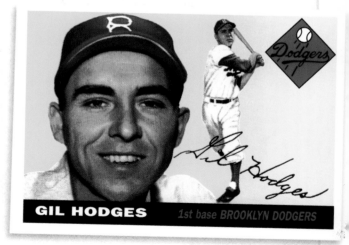

GIL HODGES   1st base BROOKLYN DODGERS

Roy Campanella
and Don Newcombe

49 Don Newcombe

Baseball's first exceptional African-American pitcher stood 6-foot-4, weighed 220 pounds, and had a fastball as good as any in the game. "Newk" was signed by the Dodgers as a free agent in 1949 and threw a shutout in his first start. From there, he became an integral part of the franchise during its "Boys of Summer" era.

Newcombe is the only player to win the Rookie of the Year, Most Valuable Player, and Cy Young awards in his career. Not only could he pitch — Newcombe's best season was 1956, when he went 27–7 — but he could hit, too. Newk was a lifetime .271 hitter.

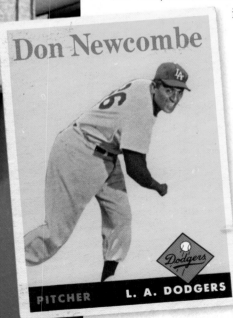

"[Newcombe's] explosive fastball was likened by Ted Williams to those of AL stars Bob Feller and Virgil Trucks."

— BaseballLibrary.com

50 The Move West

The landscape of major-league baseball and professional sports changed forever in 1957 when Dodgers owner Walter O'Malley traded Brooklyn's minor-league team in Fort Worth, Texas, for the Chicago Cubs' Pacific Coast League team in Los Angeles. The trade allowed O'Malley, who wanted but wasn't getting a new stadium in Brooklyn, to move his team west and reshape the geography of American professional sports — and forever tarnish his name in Brooklyn. The Dodgers played to a packed house on opening day, 1958 — a record home-opener crowd of 78,672 — and made their home in Los Angeles Memorial Coliseum until they moved to Dodger Stadium in 1962.

51 Taking Flight

The Dodgers became the first major-league baseball team to own its own plane, taking ownership — and flight — on January 4, 1957.

"Where would baseball be...if it didn't move west? O'Malley not only opened up the West for baseball, he opened it up for all sports."

— Red Barber in the *New York Post*

52 The Interlocking LA

It's immediately recognizable around the world, much like the New York Yankees' famous NY. When Walter O'Malley bought the minor-league Los Angeles Angels, the team had two caps: one with the letters interlocking and one with them side by side. O'Malley liked the interlocking look, and it has lasted for nearly 50 years.

53 Three for Three

The Fall Classic was played on the West Coast for the first time in 1959, and the Dodgers, who had been a disappointment in their first season out of Brooklyn, cemented their place in Southern California by beating the Chicago White Sox 4 games to 2. Despite losing Game 1, 11–0, the Dodgers — behind MVP relief pitcher Larry Sherry — gradually wore down the Sox. Youngsters Don Drysdale and Sandy Koufax got their first exposure to post-season baseball, setting the stage for what would be a glorious run into the mid-1960s.

In 1963, after having lost six of the seven World Series they'd played against the New York Yankees, the Dodgers struck back with a sweep against the boys from the Bronx. The tone was set immediately when Koufax struck out the first five batters he faced in Game 1 at Yankee Stadium. Koufax then closed out the Series with a 2–1 victory in Game 4.

Two years later, in 1965, it looked for a while as if the Minnesota Twins were going to make their first World Series appearance a victorious one. The Twins won the first two games against the Dodgers, but the advantage didn't last. Koufax again played hero for the Dodgers, pitching a three-hit shutout in Game 7 on just two days' rest to give Los Angeles its third World Series title in seven years.

54 Dodger Stadium

Like Dodger blue and the familiar LA logo, Dodger Stadium, the team's home since 1962, is an instantly recognizable symbol of the franchise. It is the essence of what a baseball park should be. With more than 3,400 trees on its 300 acres and a full-time staff of gardeners keeping it manicured, Dodger Stadium still maintains its freshness though it is approaching its 50th birthday in 2012. While the Dodgers have played eight World Series in their home park, they've shared it with many others, ranging from the Beatles to Pope John Paul II to Michael Jackson.

Walter Alston and Chuck Dressen celebrate 1959 World Series victory.

55 Walter Alston

He was hired as manager in 1954 and for the next 23 seasons—working on a one-year contract every season—led the Dodgers to 2,042 victories and four world championships. He won seven NL pennants with his smooth, understated style, which came to be known as "the Dodger way." It earned Alston a spot in the Baseball Hall of Fame.

56 Jim Gilliam

"Junior" succeeded Jackie Robinson at second base in 1953 and remained with the Dodgers through 1978. A versatile leadoff hitter, Gilliam was the National League Rookie of the Year in 1953 and played 14 years with the Dodgers, helping them win seven pennants. After he retired as a player, Gilliam remained on the coaching staff for 12 more seasons, winning three more pennants in Dodger blue.

"He didn't hit with power, he had no arm, and he couldn't run. But he did the little things to win ballgames. He never griped or complained. He was one of the most unselfish ballplayers I know."

—Walter Alston on Jim Gilliam

57 Pete Richert's Debut

Making his first appearance in the majors, the left-handed relief pitcher struck out the first six Cincinnati batters he faced, including four in one inning—one strikeout victim reached first on a passed ball—on April 12, 1962.

58 Dodger Dogs

Perhaps the most famous hot dogs in sports, nearly two million are sold each year at Dodger Stadium, where fans line up to get the foot-long dogs wrapped in a steamed bun. They can thank Thomas Arthur, the former concessions manager at the stadium, for creating the culinary classic.

Dodgers pitchers Don Drysdale, Pete Richert, Stan Williams, Sandy Koufax, and Johnny Podres

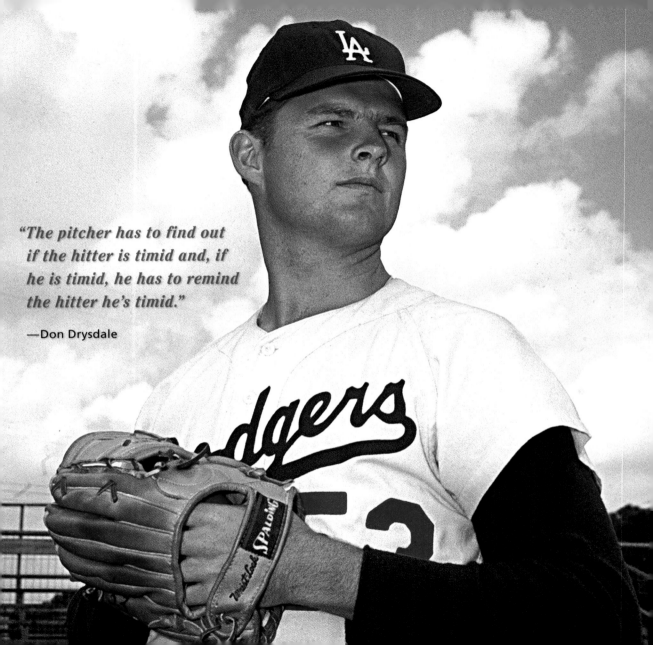

"*The pitcher has to find out if the hitter is timid and, if he is timid, he has to remind the hitter he's timid.*"

—Don Drysdale

59 Don Drysdale

Few pitchers have been more intimidating than No. 53 was. In addition to his skill and power, Drysdale wasn't afraid to be aggressive on the mound, believing the plate belonged to him, not the hitter. That explains why he hit a record 154 batters in his career.

In tandem with Sandy Koufax, Drysdale was part of one of baseball's best pitching combinations. Drysdale received the Cy Young award in 1962 after winning 25 games, and he had a stretch of 200-plus strikeouts in six of seven seasons, from 1959 to 1965. He wasn't bad with the bat, either, hitting seven home runs in 1958.

60 The Drysdale Streak

In 1968, Drysdale set a modern-day record by pitching 58 2/3 consecutive scoreless innings. It had its share of controversy, however. On May 31, Drysdale's streak appeared to be over when he hit San Francisco's Dick Dietz with a pitch with the bases loaded. However, umpire Harry Wendelstedt ruled that Dietz had made no effort to avoid being hit, Dietz' at bat continued, and he subsequently popped out. Drysdale then induced the next two batters into outs, and the shutout streak continued. Drysdale pitched six consecutive shutouts during his remarkable streak.

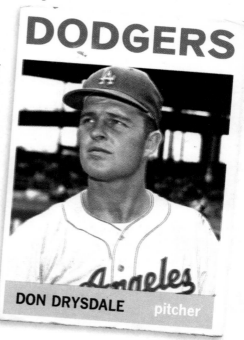

DODGERS

DON DRYSDALE — pitcher

61 Vin Scully

He is the voice of the Dodgers and has been for nearly six decades, but Scully is also the voice of baseball in America. With his recognizable voice and an unequaled knack for finding the right phrase at the right moment, Scully is among the most honored broadcasters in history. Not only is he in the Baseball Hall of Fame, he has a star on Hollywood's Walk of Fame.

Scully, who joined the Dodgers' broadcast team in 1950, one year out of Fordham University, was voted the top sportscaster of the 20th century by his peers in the American Sportscasters Association.

"At times I'll be listening to him and I'll think, 'Oh I wish I could call upon that expression the way he does.' He paints the picture more beautifully than anyone who's ever called a baseball game."

—Dick Enberg

62 Jaime Jarrin

The Spanish voice of the Dodgers for nearly 50 years, Jarrin has a place in the Baseball Hall of Fame as a winner of the Ford C. Frick award. Jarrin has been doing play-by-play of Dodgers games since 1973, using his smooth voice to tell the nightly story to thousands of listeners.

Jaime Jarrin and Vin Scully

63 Sandy Koufax

Any discussion of the game's greatest pitchers includes the name of Sandy Koufax. For a five-year period, in 1962–66, Koufax dominated the game as few pitchers ever have. With a ferocious fastball and a curveball that confounded hitters, Koufax had a remarkable stretch of sustained brilliance before physical problems ended his career prematurely. Koufax won 25 games three times and led the National League in earned run average five straight seasons. He set a record with 382 strikeouts in 1965, and he threw a no-hitter in four straight seasons.

At the biggest moments, Koufax was at his best. He pitched in four World Series, helping the Dodgers win two, in 1963 and 1965, and had a career earned run average of 0.95 in those games. He retired at age 31, after posting a 27–9 record in 1966, due to a circulatory ailment in his pitching arm. Five years later, Koufax became the youngest player inducted into the Baseball Hall of Fame.

"Trying to hit him was like trying to drink coffee with a fork."

—Willie Stargell

64 The K in Koufax

It's tough to be better than Sandy Koufax was on June 30, 1962. In what would be a 5–0 no-hit victory against the New York Mets, Koufax needed just nine pitches to strike out the side in the first inning.

65 Sandy's Perfect Game

Koufax was never better than he was on September 9, 1965, when he retired 27 Chicago Cubs in order for a 1–0 perfect-game victory. It wasn't a day for offense as the Dodgers managed just one hit, a seventh-inning single by Sweet Lou Johnson, who also scored the game's only run, in the fifth, after a walk and an error.

"There were no hard feelings on my part...over the years, you learn to forget things."

—John Roseboro on the Marichal incident

John Roseboro

66 John Roseboro

While the spotlight shone brighter on Sandy Koufax and Don Drysdale, it was Roseboro who crouched behind the plate for 11 years with the Dodgers, managing some of the game's legendary pitchers. Roseboro succeeded Roy Campanella as the Dodgers' catcher and went on to become a four-time All-Star, who won three World Series in his time with the Dodgers. Roseboro was also famous for being clubbed with a bat by Giants pitcher Juan Marichal, who was at bat during a game in 1965.

67 Maury Wills

It took Wills 10 years of minor-league ball before he reached the majors, but once he got there, he had a lasting impact. Wills was the greatest base stealer of his time and one of the best of all time. When he stole 104 bases in 1962, breaking Ty Cobb's long-standing record of 97, it was a monumental achievement. The National League's Most Valuable Player in 1962, Wills led the league in stolen bases six straight seasons, in 1960–65.

Maury Wills stealing second base

Rick Monday saves the flag.

68 The First Save

Dodgers pitcher Bill Singer gets credit for the first official save with his performance in a 3–2 victory over the Cincinnati Reds on April 7, 1969. Before that, saves were not an official statistic.

69 Rick Monday's Patriotic Play

Rick Monday was playing in the outfield for the Chicago Cubs during a visit to Dodger Stadium on April 25, 1976. When Monday saw two spectators attempting to burn the American flag in the outfield, he swooped in and saved the flag, an act that drew international attention and made Monday a hero to millions. The next month, at a game in Chicago, Dodgers executive Al Campanis presented the flag to him. Evidently Monday made quite an impression on the Dodgers' brass: they traded for him the following year.

70 Rick Monday's Home Run

It was Game 5 in the 1981 National League Championship Series, and the Dodgers were tied 1–1 with Montreal in the top of the ninth inning. With two out, Monday swatted a solo home run, which was the difference in the Dodgers' 2–1 victory, sending Los Angeles to the World Series.

71 Tommy John Surgery

It's familiar now that it's saved so many pitching careers, but when Dr. Frank Jobe did experimental surgery on Dodgers pitcher Tommy John in 1974, it was anything but routine. Jobe transplanted a tendon from John's right forearm into his left elbow, and 18 months later John was pitching again, his career saved by the innovative procedure.

"When they operated, I told them to put in a Koufax fastball. They did—but it was Mrs. Koufax's."

—Tommy John

72 The Great Infield

It was a way of life for the Dodgers— Steve Garvey at first base, Davey Lopes at second, Bill Russell at shortstop, and Ron Cey at third. They took the field together for the first time on June 13, 1973, and stayed together as an infield for more than eight years, helping the Dodgers win their first World Series title in 16 years, in 1981.

TOMMY JOHN

DODGERS

PITCHER

Cindy, Krisha, and Steve Garvey

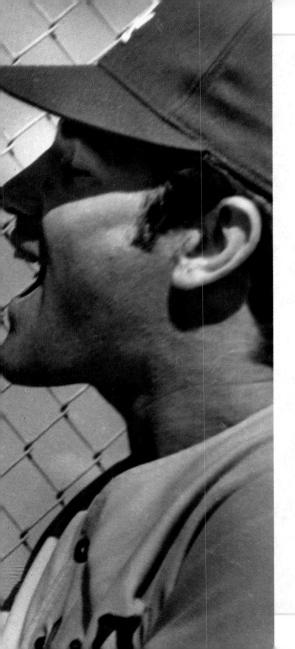

73 Steve Garvey

He was almost too perfect. Or so it seemed. With his strong jaw and handsome face, Garvey had the look of a movie star and the talent to make him a huge star. He set records for games played, hit .300 or better seven times, won four Gold Gloves, collected 200 or more hits six times, and was twice named the Most Valuable Player in the National League Championship Series.

A meticulous manager of his image, Garvey even took out a full-page ad to thank Dodgers fans for their support when he returned as a member of the San Diego Padres in 1983. Ultimately, though, Garvey's image took a serious hit when it was revealed he had fathered several children out of wedlock.

74 Garvey's Streak

He was a fixture at first base, playing 1,104 consecutive games there for the Dodgers in 1975–82. Ultimately, Garvey's streak reached 1,207 games — a National League record — before it ended when he dislocated a finger in a collision with Atlanta pitcher Pascual Perez.

75 Tommy Lasorda

For parts of seven decades, "Tommy Lasagna" has bled Dodger blue and injected the franchise with a zest for life. Lasorda, who shared his passion for food, particularly pasta, with the world, spent 20 seasons as the Dodgers manager, from late 1976 to mid-1996. Under Lasorda, the Dodgers won eight division titles and two World Series as he used his rah-rah style to motivate his players.

A lifetime baseball man, Lasorda became the game's de facto ambassador. He also managed the United States team to its first gold medal in baseball during the 2000 Sydney Olympics.

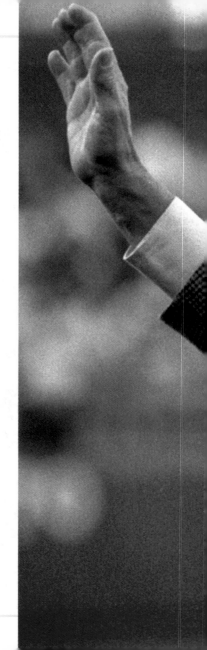

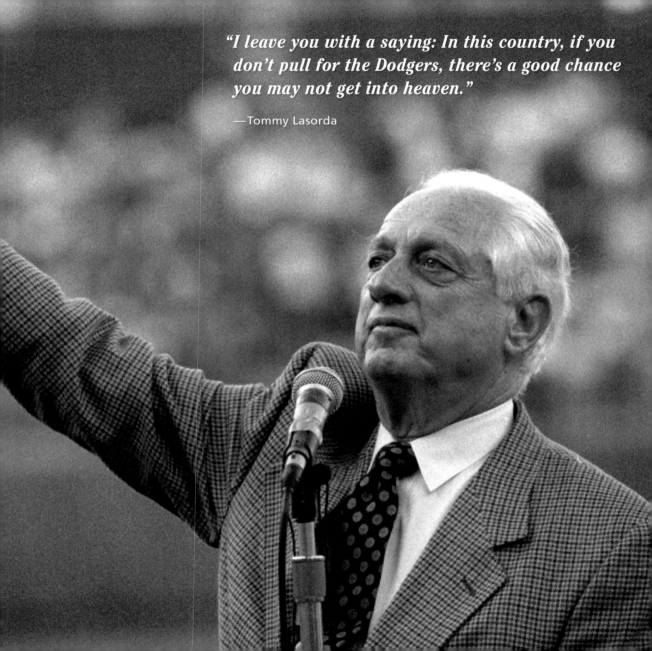

"*I leave you with a saying: In this country, if you don't pull for the Dodgers, there's a good chance you may not get into heaven.*"

—Tommy Lasorda

76 Don Sutton

He was always there. Sutton pitched 23 years in the major leagues starting in 1966, 16 of them with the Dodgers, and he never missed a scheduled start. His place in the Baseball Hall of Fame was cemented on career numbers that illuminate his endurance and consistency. Sutton won 324 games and had 3,574 career strikeouts. In 21 seasons, Sutton won 11 games or more, and he pitched five one-hitters. Although Sutton never won a Cy Young award, he pitched in four All-Star games and has the distinction of having beaten every major-league team, with a curveball his signature pitch.

77 Willie Davis

For most of his 18-year career in the 1960s and '70s, Davis roamed center field for the Dodgers, where he became as familiar as Dodger blue. Blessed with speed, Davis stole 20 or more bases in 11 consecutive seasons with the Dodgers. He also had a franchise-record 31-game hitting streak, and when he retired, Davis' 2,237 games in center field were the third most in major league history.

Willie Davis

Don Sutton

Steve Yeager congratulates Bob Welch after Game 2 of the 1978 World Series.

78 The 1977 Power Surge

The Dodgers became the first team in history to have four players hit at least 30 home runs in the same season. Steve Garvey clubbed 33 homers, Reggie Smith had 32, and Ron Cey and Dusty Baker poked 30 apiece.

79 Striking Out Reggie

It was a classic confrontation. One year after Reggie Jackson hit three home runs in Game 6 to help the New York Yankees win the 1977 World Series, Mr. October was at the plate again facing the Dodgers. Los Angeles had already won Game 1 when rookie Bob Welch stared in at Jackson in the ninth inning, with the game on the line. The Dodgers led 4–3, but the Yankees had two men on and it felt as if the world were watching. After working the count to 3-and-2, Jackson fouled off three straight pitches before striking out with a mighty cut at a Welch fastball, giving the Dodgers a Series lead of 2 games to none. That was as good as it would get for the Dodgers, who lost the next four games to the Yankees.

80 Dodgers vs. Yankees

Eleven different times the Dodgers and Yankees have met in the Fall Classic, providing some of the most memorable matchups and greatest moments in World Series history. The Yankees have won the Series eight times, but the Dodgers won their first title in 1955 by besting the Yankees in seven games, and they took the most recent showdown in 1981. Among the highlights through the years were Sandy Amoros' remarkable rally-killing catch in 1955, Sandy Koufax' brilliance in the Dodgers' 1963 sweep, Don Larsen's perfect game against the Dodgers in 1956, and Reggie Jackson's three home runs against LA in 1977.

81 The '80s Decade

The decade that gave us *Flashdance*, compact discs, and *Cheers* was good to the Dodgers. They won 825 games in 10 years, taking the 1981 and 1988 World Series while capturing the National League West title in '81, '83, '85, and '88.

82 The Penguin

They called Ron Cey "the Penguin" because he was short and stocky and wasn't the most graceful Dodger on the base paths. But Cey was beloved. For more than a decade, the third baseman played for the Dodgers, where he was a six-time All-Star who finished his career with 316 home runs. Cey's toughness was exemplified in Game 5 of the 1981 World Series when he was beaned by Yankees pitcher Goose Gossage in a frightening episode. Cey returned in Game 6 and wound up as co-MVP of the Series with teammate Steve Yeager.

Dusty Baker, Davey Lopes, and Ron Cey

Fernando Valenzuela

83 Fernandomania

On opening day in 1981, scheduled starter Jerry Reuss couldn't go, so rookie Fernando Valenzuela was handed the ball. The 20-year-old shut out the Houston Astros 2–0, the first of eight straight wins Valenzuela posted to start the season. The country was captivated by the Dodgers' new star, who looked skyward as he began his delivery. His signature pitch, "Fernando's Fadeaway," or screwball, helped Valenzuela win the Rookie of the Year award and become the first rookie to win the Cy Young award as he helped the Dodgers win the World Series.

84 Zeroes

In May 1983, the Dodgers strung together three straight shutouts. The streak started when Bob Welch won a 2–0 decision over the New York Mets. Fernando Valenzuela followed with a 5–0 win over Philadelphia, and Alejandro Pena tacked on the third blank job with a 4–0 win over the Phillies.

85 K-Mart

Fernando Valenzuela was dazzling in the 1984 All-Star Game, striking out future Hall of Famers Dave Winfield, Reggie Jackson, and George Brett in the fourth inning. It came 50 years after Carl Hubbell's famous feat of five straight All-Star strikeouts.

86 1988

Almost no one gave the Dodgers a chance when the 1988 season began, with many experts picking them to finish last in the National League West. Instead, the Dodgers produced a year to remember, winning the division, bumping off the heavily favored New York Mets in the NLCS, and, ultimately, beating the Oakland A's in the World Series, 4 games to 1.

87 Orel Hershiser's Streak

With pitcher-turned-announcer Don Drysdale watching him, Hershiser set baseball's all-time consecutive-scoreless-innings record by stringing together 59 straight shutout innings in 1988, the last 10 on September 28. Hershiser broke Drysdale's record by one-third of an inning and went on to win the Cy Young award that season.

"When you're a 17th-round draft pick, you listen to the coaches, hang around successful guys, figure out why they're successful, and emulate them."

—Orel Hershiser

Orel Hershiser

Kirk Gibson

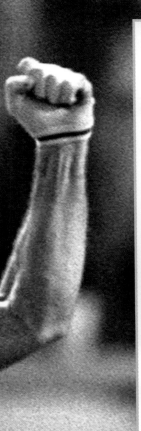

88 LA Sports' Greatest Moment

That's what Kirk Gibson's memorable Game 1 home run in the 1988 World Series was voted. The Dodgers were down 4–3 when the injured Gibson limped to the plate as a pinch-hitter to face A's ace Dennis Eckersley in the bottom of the ninth. In a moment straight out of Hollywood, Gibson ripped a home run that rocked Dodger Stadium—and the image of Gibson trotting around the bases, pulling his arm back as he ran, remains one of the Series' most memorable images. Oakland never recovered and lost the Series in five games. It was Gibson's only plate appearance in the Series.

"All year long they looked to him [Gibson] to light the fire and all year long he answered the demands. High fly ball to right field. She is gone! In a year that has been so improbable, the impossible has happened."

—Vin Scully's call of Gibson's home run

89 Rookie League

The Dodgers have owned the National League Rookie of the Year award through the years. Starting in 1979, the Dodgers won the award four straight years, with Rick Sutcliffe, Steve Howe, Fernando Valenzuela, and Steve Sax picking up the honor. In the 1990s, the Dodgers produced five straight award winners, starting with Eric Karros in '92, followed by Mike Piazza, Raul Mondesi, Hideki Nomo, and Todd Hollandsworth.

90 Sweet Success

What the pennants didn't say, the *SportsBusiness Journal* did in 1998 when it named the Dodgers the "most successful organization in Major League Baseball during the 20th century," based on on-field success, ticket sales, and marketing.

Eric Karros, Mike Piazza,
Raul Mondesi, Hideki Nomo,
and Todd Hollandsworth

91 Mike Piazza

With movie-star looks and Hall of Fame talent, Piazza became an instant star for the Dodgers when he hammered 35 home runs and drove in 112 runs in his rookie season in 1993. For five and a half seasons, Piazza was the face of the Dodgers, highlighted by his 1997 season, when he hit .362 and 40 homers and had a .638 slugging percentage.

"I long for the days when athletes were revered. I want to see the romance return to sports, to see people enjoy the game purely for the game and the players."

—Mike Piazza

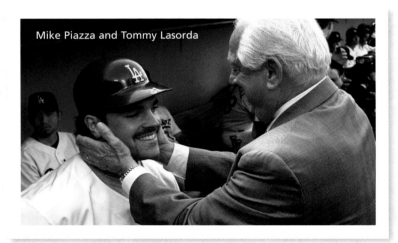

Mike Piazza and Tommy Lasorda

92 Martinez Ks 18

On June 4, 1990, Ramon Martinez tied Sandy Koufax' franchise record by striking out 18 Atlanta Braves.

93 Grand Opening

The 1999 season started with a bang—actually, two of them—compliments of Raul Mondesi. With the Dodgers trailing Arizona 6–3 with two out in the bottom of the ninth on opening day, Mondesi sent the game to extra innings with a three-run homer. Two innings later, he provided the encore—a two-out, two-run homer for an 8–6 Dodgers win.

94 Great Names

Sweetbreads Bailey, Lady Baldwin, Boom-Boom Beck, Frenchy Bordagaray, Oyster Burns, Kiki Cuyler, Fats Dantonio, Pea Ridge Day, Wheezer Dell, Cozy Dolan, Snooks Dowd, Bull Durham, Ox Eckhardt, Kid Elberfeld, Bunny Fabrique, Welcome Gaston, Mudcat Grant, Binky Jones, Candy Lachance, Rabbit Maranville, Wally Moon, Boots Poffenberger, Rip Repulski, Schoolboy Rowe, Possum Whitted, and Kaiser Wilhelm.

Raul Mondesi

Ramon Martinez

95 Feeling Green

Shawn Green set a club record in 2001 when he belted 49 home runs. A year later, Green hit 42 homers to become the first Dodger to have consecutive 40-home-run seasons.

96 Feeling Greener

There are good days, there are great days, and then there are days like the one Shawn Green had on May 23, 2002. That's when he hit four home runs and went six-for-six in a 16–3 victory over the Brewers. In addition to his four homers, Green had a single and a double, giving him a major-league-record 19 total bases.

Green wasn't finished, though. The next day he had two singles and another home run, giving him 25 total bases in two games, tying a record. And one day later, Green hit two more homers for seven in three games, another record.

"What makes him good is that he's always working, hitting all the time in the off-season. He's a lot stronger than he looks."

—Dan Naulty on Shawn Green

Nomar Garciaparra

97 The Closer

Eric Gagne was perfect in 2003. Fifty-five times he was put into save situations, and 55 times Gagne closed out the victory for the Dodgers, becoming the franchise's first Cy Young winner since 1988. He was the closest thing baseball had to a guarantee, eventually stretching his streak of consecutive saves to 84.

98 Un-four-gettable

The finale of a crucial four-game series versus the Padres at Dodger Stadium in mid-September of 2006 was a game for the ages. The Padres had won the previous two games to take a half-game lead in the division. San Diego scored two runs in the eighth inning, and three more in the ninth to build a 9–5 lead. But the Dodgers refused to fold. Jeff Kent opened the bottom of the ninth with a home run off San Diego's Jon Adkins, to close the gap to three. J.D. Drew followed with another homer off Adkins. Russell Martin and Marlon Anderson then went deep on the first two pitches thrown by Trevor Hoffman. Incredibly, the Dodgers had come back to tie the game on four consecutive solo home runs.

The Padres plated another run in the top of the tenth to once again take the lead. But in the bottom of the inning, Kenny Lofton drew a leadoff walk. Nomar Garciaparra then ended one of the most stirring and remarkable games in Dodgers history with a walk-off homer for an 11–10 Dodgers victory.

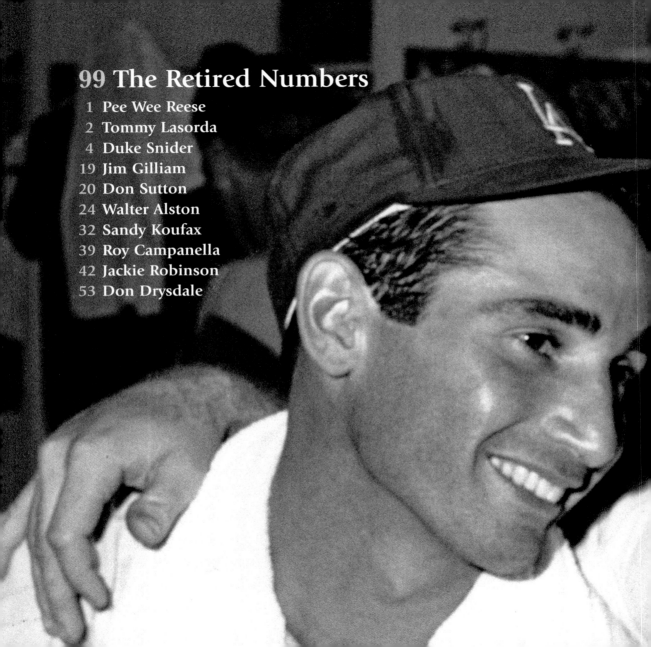

99 The Retired Numbers

1 Pee Wee Reese
2 Tommy Lasorda
4 Duke Snider
19 Jim Gilliam
20 Don Sutton
24 Walter Alston
32 Sandy Koufax
39 Roy Campanella
42 Jackie Robinson
53 Don Drysdale

Sandy Koufax and Don Drysdale

Kirk Gibson, 1988 NLCS

100 21 Pennants

The Dodgers have won the National League title 21 times in nine different decades. They have flags for 1890, 1899, 1900, 1916, 1920, 1941, 1947, 1949, 1952, 1953, 1955, 1956, 1959, 1963, 1965, 1966, 1974, 1977, 1978, 1981, and 1988.

101 Six World Championships

1955, 1959, 1963, 1965, 1981, and 1988. And counting.

Dodgers celebrating their
1955 World Series victory

Acknowledgments

This begins with words of thanks to Leslie Stoker, Jennifer Levesque, Kate Norment, Richard Slovak, and the other good people at Stewart, Tabori & Chang, where they believe in the power and pleasure of good books.

Also, a special thanks to Mary Tiegreen, whose vision has led to the creation of this book and others like it. She understands that baseball teams are more than franchises. They are a part of people's lives, one of the threads that make up the fabric of a community that reaches beyond city limits.

Again, thanks to my brother, Dave, who brought this all together and excels in the magic of creating art.

To Kevin O'Sullivan and associates at AP Wideworld Photos, and Pat Kelly and the staff at the National Baseball Hall of Fame Library; your time and efforts are greatly appreciated.

To my wife, Tamera, and my daughter, Molly; my parents, Ron and Beth Green; my sister, Edie, and the McGlone family as well as the Macchias and Brad Caplanides, whose allegiances range from the Phillies to the Mets; there aren't enough thanks.

And, finally, to the Dodgers and their worldwide web of fans, who live in a world where the sky is forever Dodger blue.

At left, Brian Jordan and Eric Karros

 **A Tiegreen Book**

Published in 2007 by Stewart, Tabori & Chang
An imprint of Harry N. Abrams, Inc.

Library of Congress Cataloging-in-Publication Data

Green, Ron, 1956-
  101 reasons to love the Dodgers /
  by Ron Green.
    p. cm.
    IISBN-13: 978-1-58479-565-0
    ISBN-10: 1-58479-565-4
  1. Los Angeles Dodgers (Baseball team)—Miscellanea.
  2. Brooklyn Dodgers (Baseball team)—Miscellanea. I. Title.
  II. Title: One hundred one reasons to love the Dodgers. III.
  Title: One hundred and one reasons to love the Dodgers.

GV875.L6G74 2007
796.357'640979494—dc22
2006028603

Text copyright © 2007 Ron Green, Jr.
Compilation copyright © 2007 Mary Tiegreen

Editor: Jennifer Levesque
Designer: David Green, Brightgreen Design
Production Manager: Alexis Mentor

101 Reasons to Love the Dodgers is a book in the 101 REASONS TO LOVE™ Series.

101 REASONS TO LOVE™ is a trademark of Mary Tiegreen and Hubert Pedroli.

Printed and bound in China
10 9 8 7 6 5 4 3 2 1

HNA

harry n. abrams, inc.
a subsidiary of La Martinière Groupe

115 West 18th Street
New York, NY 10011
www.hnabooks.com

Photo Credits

Pages 1, 2-3, 10 (inset), 16, 25, 26, 27, 28, 31, 33, 34-35, 35 (inset), 36, 38, 40, 41 (inset), 42-43, 44 (inset), 44-45, 47, 48, 50, 51, 52-53, 55, 58, 61, 64-65, 66, 68, 69, 70, 73, 75, 76-77, 78, 79, 81, 83, 84, 86, 87, 88, 89, 90, 91, 92, 94 (inset), 95, 96, 99, 100-101, 102-103, 104, 105, 106, 107, 109, 110, 112-113, 114-115, 116-117, and 118 courtesy of AP/Wide World Photos

Pages 4 (card), 9, 24 (card), 54 (magazine cover), 56, 57 (card), 59 (card), 63, 67 (card), 71 (card), 74 (ball), and 82 (card) courtesy of David Green, Brightgreen Design

Pages 12-13, 13 (card), 18 (card), 19, 21, 23 and 120 (card), courtesy of the Library of Congress Prints and Photographs Division

Pages 6-7, 8, 11, 22 (inset), 29, and 37 courtesy of the National Baseball Hall of Fame Library

Pages 14-15 courtesy of Andy Jurinko

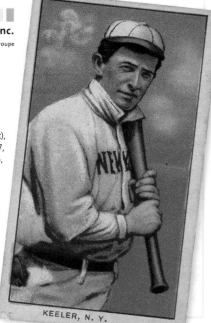

KEELER, N. Y.